Copyright © 2025 by Kelsey Pilling

All rights reserved.

No portion of this book may be reproduced in any form without written permission from the publisher or author, except as permitted by U.S copyright law.

Contents

Dedication	1
Introduction	2
Epigraph	3
1. Loss	5
2. Love	67
3. Life	123
Epilogue	199
About the Author	201

To my daughters and sons,

May you always trust your strength to rise, no matter the struggle. You are capable of more than you realize.

To my love,

Thank you for showing me how to love and be loved.

Introduction

In the spaces between loss and love, heartache and healing, we uncover the truth of what it means to be human. *The Gravity of Becoming* invites you on a journey through these shifting emotional landscapes—spaces that define us, break us, and ultimately shape us into who we are meant to be.

Like the natural world, where seasons shift and rivers carve new paths, my poetry draws inspiration from nature's elements, solitude, travel, and the connections made throughout life's journey.

Each page offers a place of transformation, reflection, and growth, where metaphors express emotions too vast for words alone, bridging the human experience with the world around us.

These pages are written with the belief that beauty rises from our most vulnerable moments. Through loss, we discover the power of life. Through heartache, we find resilience. Through love, we understand that healing is a journey—an unfolding path leading us to the person we are becoming.

May these words remind you that you are never alone in your journey. The pain, joy, and every moment in between move to the same rhythm. There is always renewal, always the promise of becoming.

Enjoy the journey.

The Guest House

This being human is a guest house.
Every morning a new arrival.

A joy, a depression, a meanness
some momentary awareness comes
as an unexpected visitor.

Welcome and entertain them all.
Even if they're a crowd of sorrows
who violently sweep your house
empty of its furniture
still, treat each guest honorably.
They may be clearing you out
for some new delight.

The dark thought, the shame, the malice
meet them at the door laughing
and invite them in.

Be grateful for whoever comes
because each has been sent
as a guide from beyond.

— Jalaluddin Rumi

KELSEY PILLING

Loss

Mourning & Memories

In the depths of the ocean

where water swallows all sound,

a heart beats with stories

aching to break the surface.

Time may soften the tales

but memories cling unyielding.

Tears give birth to waves of grief,

winding through the darkness

where sorrow drifts in its depths.

The world moves on,

days slip quietly past

but the ache remains

gnawing

relentless

an anchor that drags

through the waters of time.

. . .

THE GRAVITY OF BECOMING

And so

I bear the weight,

a vessel of what was,

a burden no time can lift.

With grief caught in my sails,

this ache I will carry

as the winds keep guiding me home.

— Enduring Ache

There's a quiet knowing

we remain woven,

even as time unravels

the threads between us.

The roads we once travelled

hum with our voices,

their echoes lingering

soft

but near.

In quiet reflection

I return to the place

where affection once bloomed,

now a garden of stories

with roots deep in memory.

. . .

Yet even in the fading,

what we were still lingers

not as love

but as traces of stars

scattered in the vastness of the sky.

It's not about holding on

but remembering

the way we existed,

beautiful and haunting,

like the ghost of a love once alive.

— Traces of Stars

Your presence feels miles away,
though you lie beside me
your body is motionless,
lost in a trance I can't reach.

The warmth we once shared
fades into the darkness,
as night thickens with silence
and laughter drifts like a distant breeze.

I search for traces
of the love we once knew,
reaching for memories
that slip through my fingers.

Though you're here beside me
your heart has already parted,
as the space between us
stretches too far to reach.

. . .

I close my eyes

but sleep eludes me,

wandering in the emptiness

of a love that once was whole.

Tonight

I sleep alone,

drifting as the ghost of us,

where silence casts its shadow

deep into the bones of our past.

— Lonely

Do you ever notice

a presence in the air?

Someone else is sitting

in my rocking chair.

The same chair that cradled our baby,

that felt my final embrace,

now sways for another

filling the void

that you replaced.

— Ghost

Time stretches between us,

yet our threads remain knotted.

Tangled with a love

from a story left undone,

from lovers

to enemies

now strangers

with memory.

— Tangled Threads

What is health when it's no longer here?

What is life when there's nothing to fear?

What is time when the clock disappears?

What is forever when there are no more years?

— Death's Door

THE GRAVITY OF BECOMING

Every full moon

I shed another layer of you,

like a snake slipping from its skin

and tides pulled clean from the shore.

The mountains stand unchanged

but the landscape shifts beneath my feet.

With every full moon

I lose a little more of you.

— Release

Waiting in the shadows

of what used to be,

chasing illusions

that can't be seen.

Running from the future

while clinging to the past,

too stubborn to admit

this love wouldn't last.

Promises scattered

like leaves in the breeze,

drifting away

while fading in the trees.

The laughter we shared

now echoes in vain,

a bittersweet melody

singing with pain.

. . .

THE GRAVITY OF BECOMING

Through heartache

we learn to become whole,

as strength grows

we release control.

One step forward

brings two steps back,

building abundance

from memories of lack.

Our story was written in the sand,

each grain slipping through our hands.

I walk toward a future

no longer entwined,

with the sand beneath my feet

I finally leave you behind.

— Written in the Sand

They say sorrow is a season
and winter always turns to spring
but my branches stand bare
with my leaves lost to the wind.

I know I should let go
but my heart still clings,
trapped in December
while longing for June.

Memories of you
drift like snow in the air,
cold
weightless
impossible to bear.

Through every winter
I'm lost in the snow,
trapped in the past
of love long ago.

. . .

Frozen in time

where the cold lingers deep,

waiting for spring

to thaw what remains.

— Lost in December

I held your hand during your last breath

two strangers in body, two souls in death,

one heart let go, fading into the night

while the other remained between darkness and light.

One soul was carried to the other side

while the other stood where life and death collide,

as seasons shift and daylight wanes

logic bends where time remains.

There is no life without death's embrace,

no path forward without something erased,

all things end like autumn leaves

whispering truth among the breeze.

They say grief softens as seasons turn

but some sorrows settle, too deep to unlearn.

— Crossing Over

THE GRAVITY OF BECOMING

I imagine my eyes brimming

like a glacial lake swelling in spring,

grief and gratitude

rising as one.

Your presence weighs heavy

while your absence endures.

I cradle both joy and sorrow

as the past drifts through the present,

a tide that never fully recedes.

Time bends

but never breaks.

I will carry you still,

not in longing

but in the countless shades

of what we were,

what we are

and what we'll never be.

— To See You Again

I've learned to rest

in the weight of being lost,

to let the unknown cradle me,

a cocoon before daybreak.

Beyond the hush of midnight

where darkness unravels

and doubt dissolves,

a new version of me

is already reaching

for the light.

— Metamorphosis

THE GRAVITY OF BECOMING

My tears

map the sky,

constellations

scattering

like shattered light.

While my chest

swells

under the weight

of collapsing stars.

— Celestial Grief

In the dark

where shadows stretch long,

a hollow chest quivers

beneath the weight

of what is gone.

The air is thick with memories,

mourning what will never return,

hope unravels

and grief weaves its roots.

But deep in the soil

of what was,

resilience stirs

in a hollow chest,

a breath that bends

but does not break.

. . .

Through the ache

resilience blooms,

even on the loneliest nights

the moon still rises.

— Inner Strength

My mind shields my heart from pain,

burying memories

too dark to face.

But silence speaks heavy in its grip,

as my bones bear the weight

of remembrance.

Shame sinks beneath the surface,

swallowed

by the will to endure.

But even as darkness lingers,

light is bound

to break.

. . .

Decades pass, yet you walk free,

a monster of a man

still roaming the streets.

While I gather the scattered pieces of me,

I trust that justice

will speak.

You will have your judgment day,

and I,

I will reclaim my peace.

— Karmic Justice

When you look into darkness

it looks back at you,

with eyes weighted

by all you've endured.

It stirs in the shadows

telling tales of the deep,

where secrets lie dormant

and forgotten memories sleep.

The longer you stare

the further it reaches,

unearthing the pieces

you thought you'd never see.

As the shadows watch

you start to understand,

darkness is not just a place

but a part of your own hand.

. . .

It is there to teach you

to face what you can't outrun,

to heal what you can't hide

and illuminate what's undone.

When you look at darkness

know it sees all that you are,

reflecting every fear

and every hidden scar.

When you look at darkness

it is not just a view,

it's a mirror to your depths,

exposing what is true.

— Shadow Work

My chest aches for warmth forgotten

as my eyes mourn skies once wide

and clouds of rippling satin drift

where the cold wind runs to hide.

I dream of hues that kiss the earth,

of petals spun in golden light,

where open fields

exhale in song

and stars weave silver

through the night.

I ache for days that linger long,

where shadows break

and rivers rise,

as mountains wake to birds in flight

wrapped in the arms

of endless skies.

. . .

THE GRAVITY OF BECOMING

When all things fade

to rise anew,

I'll wait

forever

here for you.

— Summer

Letting go of someone
you thought would stay forever,
is never easy.

Living in the wake of their absence
feels like carrying shadows,
tracing the ghost of a life
that no longer exists.

Hope fades with the wind,
dissolving into the ether,
loosening seams of certainty
and unravelling the fabric of peace.

Release them,
as hard as it is.

. . .

THE GRAVITY OF BECOMING

They walked away.

And so did you,

for reasons understood.

Some people change.

But most

are meant to drift

through our memories.

— Broken Love

You cherish the moments,
the feelings they leave behind,
but their absence weighs heavy,
an anchor pressing on your mind.

Life is neither kind
nor fair.

Some souls drift
while others stay
soft yet deep,
etched in the heart
forever to keep.

Find solace in the love once known.
Release the sorrow.
Let go of what's outgrown.
. . .

THE GRAVITY OF BECOMING

Hold tight to the memories
that shine pure and bright.

They carve themselves
into the stones of time,
leaving imprints in the wind,
turning loss into light.

— Weight

Echoes of chaos

as health retreats,

the body, a fortress

caught in defeat.

The smoke of deception

is no longer denied,

a vessel that fights

but longs for what's tried.

The mirror holds a stranger

as reflections decay,

but deep in the soul

hope can find its way.

— Resilience

THE GRAVITY OF BECOMING

Giving the wrong meaning

to wandering thoughts

can wound the mind,

warping clarity into confusion,

and fracturing light into shadows.

What festers in silence

may carve its name into you,

etching sorrow

deep into your bones

and drowning your heart

underwater.

But even pain can be reborn

from the wreckage,

like a flame that rises

from the ashes,

wild and fierce,

enduring as the dawn.

— Wounded Artist

After what feels like a lifetime,

I recall the good times

with quiet peace in my soul,

freed from the weight of old wounds.

I remember our joy

and the warmth of our laughter,

the silent moments that spoke volumes

and the love that grounded us from the clouds.

Now, I hold it all

with a lighter heart, at ease,

bathed in the grace of time,

finding peace where pain once lingered.

And though the ache has softened,

appreciation lingers,

a steady reminder

of what once was.

. . .

We were once complete,

and I carry gratitude

for every fragment of us

still broken in my chest.

— Pieces of Us

Sift through the ashes

of yesterday's warmth,

scattered by the wake

of a consuming fire.

In the fierce heat of its burn,

solace is not in fleeing

but in the weight of rising.

Not as who you were

but as a soul reframed.

Birthed through fire,

unbroken

and unstoppable.

— Phoenix Rising

At my own expense

I cling to the good in you,

cradling fragments of hope

too frail to break through,

too blind to see the fractures

splintering beneath the light.

But buried deep

in marrow and ash,

truth stirs,

unshaken and untamed.

This is the final full moon

for me to release you

to the wolves,

and let the wind

devour your name.

— Wolf Moon

Sometimes we must walk away

from all we've known,

the comfort of familiar faces,

the places we once called home,

the choices that shaped us

and the limits that confined our dreams.

It's in the bold leap into the unknown

that we uncover the fragments of ourselves buried deep,

shards of who we were,

long lost and forgotten.

Only by releasing our grasp

can we create room to claim

what was waiting,

the fire that burns with our passion,

the strength we thought we lost

and the person we are meant to become.

— Release to Receive

I've seen it with my own eyes,
felt it crawl beneath my skin,
heard it woven through your lies
and tasted the bitterness
of your sins.

Darkness speaks in spades,
lurking in each breath,
where secrets fester
fed by addiction's depth.

But even shadows yield to light,
fractured by the weight of truth,
as dawn breaks
through our goodbye.

— In Spades

How do you give when your well runs dry,

when your heart is hollow

like a wilted garden,

scarred by the weight of loss and sorrow

pressing on your chest?

Do you collect whispers from the silence

or catch the glow of distant stars

in a sky swallowed by night?

Perhaps it's in the quietest gestures,

a smile

as gentle as the first light of dawn,

or a fleeting touch

like a rainbow breaking through the rain.

. . .

From that emptiness

life begins to stir,

slowly

tenderly

a future rises,

born from the soil of pain

and nourished by the strength

that's birthed from within.

— Seeds of the Future

Walking away is not just leaving us,

it's leaving the pieces of me

carved over the years

shaped by your shadow.

It's stepping into the unknown,

trusting the pull of the stars

to guide me,

to cradle my heart

in a gentle embrace,

letting the mountains ground me

while the winds whisper of freedom.

I release what was,

unravelling the past,

the pain

and the parts of me

that were never meant to stay.

— Emergence

THE GRAVITY OF BECOMING

Some days

I feel born of the stars,

crafted from light

infinite

and boundless.

And some days

I feel condemned to darkness,

tethered to shadows

and trapped in the dusk

before daybreak.

— Starseed

It's never too late

to begin again.

To shed the weight of yesterday

and breathe life into dreams long forgotten.

You hold the pen

the power to rewrite your story,

to erase what has faded away

and sketch a path toward a future untold.

With each sunrise

a blank canvas unfolds before you,

a chance to paint the life you've always dreamed

in shades of possibility

and hope.

It's never too late.

. . .

Every ending

cradles a seed of renewal,

quietly anticipating your touch

to awaken its magic.

The future unfolds before you,

waiting for your courage to paint

with the bold strokes of your soul,

stepping fearlessly into the unknown.

— Paint the Future

When you've lost your way
sing to the rhythm of your soul
and dance beyond the weight
of fear and judgment.

Let your body break free,
unburdened by thought,
moving wildly with the dreams
of your five-year-old self.

Reconnect with the joy
of unfiltered creativity,
the boundless energy of imagination
and the freedom that once lived inside you.

Feel the pulse of wholeness
and pure expression,
as if the world was made
to be reshaped by your touch.

. . .

In those moments

you'll remember

the power to heal

to grow

and create,

has always been within you.

And when you welcome your inner child

you'll find the strength to rebuild

everything you thought you'd lost.

— The Child Within

Hatred and loathing

are not the opposite of love,

indifference is.

In hatred

there is still a connection,

a raw consuming force,

passionate

and undeniable.

In love

there is vulnerability,

an unravelling of the heart.

But indifference,

that cold, silent void

exists where nothing matters,

where even the fiercest emotion

is absent.

. . .

Indifference is the space

between what was once felt

and what is now gone.

A silence

louder than words,

where even hatred cannot reach.

— Detachment

You were a grizzly in disguise,

a teddy bear beneath the surface

wearing your scorpion as a shield,

hiding your softness

with a sting that kept the world at bay.

Grounding your stars in the roots of the earth,

buried beneath the palms,

shielded by the shell

that protected your heart.

Now you dance on the edge

of dreams and heaven,

a gentle giant

and scorpion of the sky.

— Scorpio

THE GRAVITY OF BECOMING

Her delicate frame held the soul of a warrior,

her laughter echoing through the corridors of time,

with a grace that could calm the fiercest storm.

Her love carved its path

like a river shaping stone.

Her eyes

windows to a thousand stories,

reflecting a life

lived through dreams.

As the sun rises over the horizon

she dances in the heavens,

forever guided

by the brilliance of her light.

— Irish Dancer

What we once thought was our guiding light

can sometimes lead us astray.

But in the wandering

we find there are no wrong paths,

only detours that reveal our truth.

Let go of what you think you need

and trust in what is meant to be.

Every moment

is a step closer to destiny,

leading us exactly where

we are meant to grow.

— Directions

THE GRAVITY OF BECOMING

A master of his craft,
his hands were architects of dreams,
moulding wood with patience
and precision
carving life into pieces of the earth.

A giant
in stature and in heart,
his laughter filled every room
leaving love that resonates.

In each puzzle he crafted
and every piece of timber shaped,
he built bridges to the past
and pathways to the future.

His work was a language,
a silent conversation between
earth and sky, hands and heart,
generations and time.

. . .

His legacy isn't in what he built
but in what he instilled,
purpose
strength
connection.

Though his hands have quieted
and his voice no longer lingers,
his spirit is etched into tree trunks,
woven into the fabric of the forest.

He is not gone,
he lives in every corner of our lives,
guiding us
as a steady force
and a silent hand.

. . .

Through the work he left behind,

through the love he planted,

he continues to shape the world.

A master of creation

and legacy,

forever rooted in our lives.

— Patriarch

As your body faded from this earth

your spirit rose in visions,

a quiet current of wisdom

drifting through my dreams.

One foot in the heavens,

the other in the soil,

your light weaves itself

through the fabric of the clouds.

When your spirit soared

it became a timeless seed,

a legacy entwined through the trees,

its magic rooted deep within me.

— Preservation

THE GRAVITY OF BECOMING

I stand ready for my departure.

I do not seek it, nor do I fear it

but when the time arrives

I will meet it with open arms.

Each winter, I have rehearsed

the art of letting go,

shedding what was

so something new may bloom.

I have died and been reborn

a thousand times

rising again,

like spring calling the flowers from their slumber.

— Seasons of the Soul

The smell of cedar and sage lingers in the air

as I walk our trails through the mountains.

Their peaks kiss the sky,

with cliffs that challenge the heart.

The rustle of leaves beneath my feet,

the breath of the wind through ancient trees,

the roar of the river, relentless and wild—

each sound draws me closer to you.

Sunlight filters through the branches

casting shadows like memories,

while the coolness of the earth

grounds me in moments long past.

Every step I take reminds me of our days,

the way time seemed to pause,

as if the world held its breath

in honour of the bond we shared.

. . .

Through every scent, every sound

every stone beneath my toes,

I find traces of you,

as though the land carries your essence.

And though you are gone,

these trails

these rivers

still pulse with your presence,

engraved in the bones of the earth.

— Senses

In the silent hours

I watch you fade,

as a spark swallowed

by the weight of the dark.

Chasing fleeting highs

that vanish too fast,

lost in the ghosts

of your haunted past.

Your laughter

a flicker

a flare in the night

but the chains of your prison

extinguish your light.

— Fading

THE GRAVITY OF BECOMING

I traced your name

through the dust of my memories,

but even ghosts fade

when left untouched.

Time has softened the sharp edges of grief,

and in the quiet

I've learned to live with what's vanished,

you

and the ghosts of my past.

— Remnants of You

Grief is love

with nowhere to go,

a quiet ache

that lingers slow.

But in the stillness,

they remain—

whispers of the wind,

dancing in the stars,

falling softly

with the rain.

— They Remain

Love

The depths of connection

When the road grows heavy
and the light feels far from sight,
know that we walk beside you
steadfast through the night.

Through every tear that falls
like rain upon the earth,
let the weight you bear
reveal your quiet worth.

Strength is forged in struggle
like a lotus through the mud,
your future's held in patience
as the roses wait to bud.

The winds will carry your spirit high
while your roots hold steady and strong.
Rise where love and hardship collide,
claiming the strength that was yours all along.

— Family Love

Chaotic love

is like diving headfirst into the eye of a storm,

drawn to its stillness,

mistaking it for peace.

But the moment you let down your guard

the winds shift

and chaos consumes you whole,

dragging you further

from the calm you once believed was within reach.

The storm rages,

tearing through everything you held dear,

leaving only scattered fragments

of the life you thought you knew.

Yet, in the wreckage

strength stirs as rebirth.

. . .

You are no longer at the mercy
of the storm.

You rise with the wind
lifted from the ashes of undoing,
learning
unlearning
rebuilding
piece by piece.

Through the turbulence
you push forward,
until, at last
you break through to the other side,
reaching peace beyond chaos.
. . .

THE GRAVITY OF BECOMING

And in the end

you no longer fear the storm,

you become the gentle breeze.

Not fighting

not fleeing

but growing steady in your own strength.

Knowing the true power

was never in resisting the storm

but in rising

once the winds have passed.

— Tornado Love

Once upon a time

you loved me and I loved you,

just two kids

who couldn't see it through.

To my favorite never was

as I look back in review,

I remember the hearts

that always remained true.

I see you smile

as if all is fine

but love was never realized

and it can't be defined.

I've watched the wrinkles

grace your face

as time continues

to drift away.

. . .

THE GRAVITY OF BECOMING

It's been years
since our embrace
but you keep hoping
we'll find our way.

I settle for the sadness
of parting ways,
next life we'll get it right,
we came upon that phrase.

When there are no mountains left to climb
no more battles to be fought,
when our love endures through time
and summer's breeze is soft.

Until then,
my favorite never was.

— Star Crossed

Mending a heart lost in the past

too blind to see we'd never last.

Two hearts became three

the moment you let go of me.

Love born from broken strings

was never meant to sing.

Our song was never meant to be

and our winter won't find spring.

Two hearts

became three

now one heart

is set free.

— Love Triangle

After months of tearing you

from my thoughts,

I spent years

purging my body

of the poison

from your love.

It clung to me

like acid through my veins,

until I finally learned

to let it burn.

Now, every scar left behind

is a reminder of the strength that grew

from our demise.

— Toxic Love

Do you remember the vineyard

where we danced among the vines,

laughing

playing

sipping our wine?

A bliss so pure

it couldn't be described.

Then came the fracture

where illusion split at the seams.

You weren't who you claimed to be,

just a character crafted

for me to believe.

And love unraveled

before it had begun.

Too good to be true

marked the end

of me and you.

— The Goodbye

THE GRAVITY OF BECOMING

In moments of doubt
when the light starts to fade,
I'll be your anchor
your shelter
your shade.

Your torch in the night
beneath darkened skies,
the spark in your fire,
the song in your sighs.

With fingers entwined
we'll walk the unknown
with love as our compass
you're no longer alone.

— Soul Strings

Late love

simple yet profound,

is an alchemy where two souls

find their rhythm.

No rush

no need to claim

just a quiet trust

through time's gentle unfolding.

It glows like twilight

soft and slow,

a love grounded in patience

with roots deepening in each passing moment.

Years have taught us

through silence and ease,

that hearts once shattered

are now whole—

anchored in peace.

. . .

At last

love is no longer a chase,

but a steady presence

rooted in grace,

with a quiet strength that rises

like the sun across our skies.

— Twilight Love

When the nights grow quiet

and winter lingers long

I remember our stories

and how we carried on.

Clinging to adventures

like climbers on a cliff,

nurturing our spirits

with each sacred gift.

In the forest

beneath the towering trees,

we were the roots

that gave rise

to new life.

Through seasons

we flourished and thrived,

our love rooted deep

in the life we revived.

. . .

THE GRAVITY OF BECOMING

Now, in the silence

our bond rests like stone,

planted deep in the earth

like bones buried alone.

A presence beneath the surface

anchored in time,

unseen but unforgotten,

no longer reaching for the climb.

— Buried Love

I rest my head on your shoulder

feeling the weight

of our unspoken love,

a fleeting instant that held

the gravity of lifetimes.

Classic art lined the walls

with chairs fit for kings and queens,

each piece bathed in history,

bearing the weight of untold stories.

Then came a stranger in blue suede shoes

with presence filling the room

he revealed future news,

"One day, you will marry."

The air hung heavy

as his voice anchored the room,

like a weight settling between us

in a truth long hidden, yet familiar.

. . .

THE GRAVITY OF BECOMING

In the soft glow of candlelight

the room held its breath

and time

ceased to exist.

Our future was announced

before we had even begun.

In the quiet ballroom

the walls will whisper of our love

for generations to come.

— Soul Love

When the energy of my soul

met yours,

all the walls I built

as barriers to love

crumbled beneath the gravity of your heart.

Nothing could match

our alignment.

Nothing could prevent

our connection—

not the storms of yesterday

or the shadows that dare to stretch ahead.

All that endured

was my fierce trust in you,

drawn to your open hand

welcoming me to forever.

— Destined Love

THE GRAVITY OF BECOMING

In a world of filters and curated dreams
where every pixel hides an unspoken ache,
self-doubt lingers in the space where love
is measured by likes and views.

Chasing reflections never meant to be real,
versions sculpted by enhancements that fade.
Faces adorned with fleeting trends,
bodies polished to perfection,
yet still, self-doubt finds its place.

Scrolling through galleries of flawless lives,
where true beauty hides beneath,
unseen
unspoken
and longing to be known.

Lost in borrowed light,
their essence fades further from sight.

. . .

But one day, they'll understand

beauty isn't perfection.

It's carved in the lines

etched in a face of a life well-lived.

Every mark is a testament to resilience,

every scar is a story carved through time.

True beauty is not built or bought,

it rises from within,

untouched by trends

and unphased by time.

The power of being whole lies not in conformity,

but in the courage to be unfiltered.

To stand bare before the world,

fearless in your truth.

. . .

Your worth isn't painted on your skin
or bound by numbers on a screen.
It lives in the love you offer yourself,
the light you carry despite the weights.

The road to self is long,
shaped by time and growth.
Embracing your truth
reveals a beauty deeper than mirrors.

Beauty is in your kindness,
your laughter
your light
and the fullness of your own heart.

So rise.
Let your soul be seen.
In a world of fragments,
be beautifully whole.

— Unfiltered Love

When the world feels empty

close your eyes and you will see,

I am not just this body,

this fleeting breath,

nor the ring I wear

untouched by death.

I am not only the arms

that hold you tight,

nor the lips

that kiss you goodnight.

I am the breeze

that stirs the trees,

the river's song

that meets the seas.

. . .

I am the sun

that warms your skin

and the moonlight

pulling you back within.

When this body fades away,

my love will live

beyond my grave.

— Love Beyond

In the heart of the wild, where spirits roam,
adventurers found a place to call home.
Their laughter echoed through valleys wide,
climbing mountains with the eagle as their guide.

Soaring on waves with surfboards in tow,
riding the rhythm where the tides would flow.
Salt in their hair and sun on their skin,
each day was a canvas for love to begin.

Through forests they trekked and rivers they raced,
chasing the thrill of love that couldn't be erased.
Splashing through rapids, their spirits untamed,
in the rush of the river, wild love was named.

As seasons shifted, their quests did too,
from sun-kissed days to skies of winter's blue.
Strapping on gear, they embraced the chill,
ice climbing high, awaiting the thrill.

. . .

THE GRAVITY OF BECOMING

In the backcountry snow, they measured the scales,
with laughter and warmth, they weathered the trails.
Winter camping beneath a blanket of stars,
together, they forgot the weight of their scars.

With frost in the air and a love born anew,
dreams were shared as the winter winds blew.
Through blizzards and storms, their bond only grew,
in the heart of the wild, their love stayed true.

Love as untamed as the peaks they scaled,
a force unbroken, through storms, it prevailed.
With summer's warmth and winter's embrace,
two adventurers were bound by love's fearless chase.

— Wild Love

The earth couldn't hold our love.

Like waves on the shore—

relentless, crashing,

always reaching, always pulling.

We danced in fire

with chaos as our guide,

hearts burning recklessly

wild and free.

But when lightning strikes

love's power burns—

too fierce to hold

too wild to learn.

We carried a love too vast for our bones,

too endless for time

too wild for the mind.

. . .

We burned too bright

too fierce to survive—

a blessing

a curse

too alive to thrive.

Now only shadows in the wind,

too wild

too free

too fleeting to last.

A love that can't be tamed

is a love that can't be saved.

— Aftermath

The love you deserve

will find you softly,

when your heart is still

and your spirit is free.

It will arrive gently,

not in haste,

but with patience—

a river carving its path

through the landscape of your soul.

This love will not demand

but will enter with grace,

filling the spaces where pain once lived,

mending the fractures with its quiet presence.

It will find you

when you've let go of the past,

forgiven the wounds that once held you back

and opened your heart to the beauty ahead.

. . .

The love you deserve will not rush

but bloom in its own time,

like a garden reaching for the sun,

quietly unfolding

until you realize it was always there,

waiting for the right moment

to rise.

And when it does

you will know

deep in your being,

this is the love

you were always meant to hold.

— The Love You Deserve

Where the forest hums

with the wind's sweet song,

and laughter sways,

both light and strong.

Music drifts

through endless days,

where time halts

in youth's embrace.

Bonfires glow,

their warmth ignites,

casting sparks

that dance through the night.

In golden light,

hearts intertwine,

lost in moments

that feel divine.

. . .

But seasons turn
and summer fades,
as autumn whispers
through amber glades.

Old hearts stir
with memories deep,
a love once wild
now softly sleeps.

These are the days
when hearts first knew
the fire of young love,
fierce and true.

A moment brief,
yet burning bold,
an endless story
left untold.

— Young Love

Through our connection
I found my footing,
roots pressed deep into the earth
with hands that felt its heartbeat.

Above
clouds drifted freely,
while below,
roots interlaced
and waterfalls cascaded
like sacred fountains.

The days we shared were numbered
but never counted.
Each sunrise brought new life,
each sunset,
whispered a sweet goodbye.

. . .

Our souls were set free,

untethered by time

but our hearts remained bound.

As seasons changed and colours dimmed,

our path scattered like the leaves,

but the love we once knew

rests in the breeze.

It lingers in the spaces

between breaths

and seasons,

a shadow that stretches

across years gone by,

never to return

but never to die.

— Stepping Stone Love

I long for the moments
when our hearts skipped a beat,
when our souls aligned
and we felt complete.

The shape of your face
may blur with time
but I ache for the warmth
of your sweet embrace.

I yearn for the laughter
that once filled this space,
where our worlds entwined
and love knew no end.

When you hear me
meet me at our tree,
deep in the forest
of what used to be.

. . .

I'll wait at its roots

where our echoes remain,

with our initials carved in a heart

never to fade away.

— Separation

The stars whisper truths through silence,

understood only by souls that have loved before.

A language beyond love,

beyond earth

beyond time—

written in the dark

beyond the stars.

— Soul Secrets

THE GRAVITY OF BECOMING

When you find love,
not in perfect moments,
but in the cracks where your soul feels exposed,
where vulnerability becomes strength
and tenderness flows freely
like a river after the rain.

When trust is not built on promises
but on a steady hand that never falters,
you begin to see love for what it is.
A force
gentle yet unbreakable.
A spark that lights your path
and kindles the fires deep within.

In love's quiet grace
you discover belief not only in love,
but in the goodness that often goes unnoticed,
in the kindness we forget to see
and in the profound connection that binds us all.

. . .

Love becomes the mirror

in which you see yourself anew,

not just as a lover, but as a whole being,

worthy

complete

and capable of greatness.

And as you love,

you heal

your heart rebuilding piece by piece,

until you see the world with eyes that recognize

the strength that exists in the gentlest love.

This is true love,

in its raw, authentic form.

Not something to possess

but something that embodies you,

inspires

motivates

and renews.

. . .

And when love is this real,

it makes you believe

once again,

that all things are possible.

The world can be as beautiful

as the love you thought impossible.

— Restored Love

In love there is no concept of time,

no right moment

no wrong moment

to fall.

The mind spins the illusion

of bad timing,

softening the truth

with little white lies.

This love

was never yours to hold,

and you

were never theirs to keep.

The right love arrives untethered,

unchained by moments,

unbound by time.

— Beyond Time

Your breath fills my lungs, a steady rhythm within me.

Your chords hum softly, vibrating through my veins.

Your drum steadies my heart, beating with time,

while your guitar strings strum

through the silence of the night.

Each note played becomes part of us,

love merging to shape constellations,

songs scattering stars across the heavens,

trailing light through the universe.

A rhythm as timeless as the cosmos,

woven into the symphony of existence

where every heart beats with destiny

and each pulse guides us toward infinity.

— The Rhythm of Us

I'll enter your dreams,
walking beside you through fantasies,
where the world is soft
and time slips away.

The sky will be painted
in shades of midnight
to reveal stars
only our love can see.

I'll guide you through the gardens
where each petal holds a wish
and the air hums with promises
waiting to be spoken.

In the space between breaths
we'll uncover worlds only we can name,
where love is free,
dancing wildly through the unseen.

. . .

THE GRAVITY OF BECOMING

I'll follow the glow of your creativity
and the light of my imagination,
like the moon leading us to realms
where limits cease to exist.

Together, we'll reach the stars
rising above the impossible
until our love breaks the darkness
of the sky.

Unveiling a universe
where infinity is born
and love
becomes the force
that lifts all limits.

— Pisces Love

Through your eyes,

I felt your pain

and glimpsed the quiet hope beneath.

In their depths,

I saw the future we could shape,

a life built by hearts combined.

In your hands,

I felt the gentleness

that softens the world,

and the strength that holds us

when storms ignite.

Through your heart,

I felt a love that held steady.

Our story unfolding,

page by page,

one chapter at a time.

. . .

And then

through your soul

I found my place—

not as a guest

but as part of you.

A home I hadn't sought,

yet always knew I belonged.

— Transparent Love

Express gratitude to the universe

for unseen blessings,

for quiet embers of hope

that cradle your dreams,

and the stillness that prepares your heart

for paths yet to unfold.

Blessings are on their way,

wrapped in time,

waiting to be revealed,

like the sun behind clouds.

Embrace the magic to come.

Let each breath be an offering

for the love that surrounds you

and the journey to places unimagined.

. . .

Trust the universe to guide your story,
filling your life with gifts,
both small and grand.

Open your heart to the abundance ahead
and let gratitude be the light
that guides your way.

— With Love

In the wake of countless years,

so much life was lived

beneath darkened skies.

The songs of the past hum softly,

etched in scars—

each a lesson forged in fire,

carved by the hands of time.

Yet, after every wound heals,

love returns

silent and sure,

like a rare bird finding its way home.

Time slips away as two hearts,

bound by an unseen force,

yield to the gravity pulling them closer.

. . .

In the weight of belonging, love rises—

no longer waiting

but alive,

igniting the world anew,

leaving no corner untouched by life.

— Love in Waiting

She had always been untamed,
a wild spirit dancing with the wind,
freed from the world's constraints
like a bird that could never be caged.

Independence was her rhythm,
a melody soaring through infinite skies,
never anchored, always reaching,
a heart forever chasing the horizon.

Then, his love found her—
not to bind her
but to ground her.
Rooted and boundless,
fierce as the winds,
reaching for the stars,
like the earth kissing the sky.
. . .

He offered her the strength

of steady ground,

without clipping her wings.

In his love,

she discovered balance—

the strength to stand firm

while her wings remained open.

Liberated,

yet cradled by a love

that lets her soar,

forever free.

— Wings of Love

In the stillness of mundane moments
the extraordinary reveals itself.

A glance holds galaxies,
and silence hums in sonnets
only the heart can hear.

Love is both a refuge
and a wildflower,
blooming in the cracks of our lives,
rooted in chaos,
yet endlessly alive.

Joy and sorrow intertwine—
two threads of the same cloth.

. . .

Where we are both the questions
and the answers,

the longing

and the arrival,

the breath between us

and the stillness that cradles us.

Love fills our lungs

as the destination

awakens within us.

Where we find

that we are not only

the seekers

but the found.

— Life Partners

Find your strength

not in the approval of others

but in the quiet force rising from your heart,

when all else falls away.

Find your light

not as a beacon for others

but as the fire that burns

unapologetically from within,

casting shadows on the doubts that haunt you.

Find your purpose

not in society's judgments

but in the ancient whispers

of your own heart,

guiding you toward

what only you

were born to create.

. . .

Find your love,
not as validation from without
but as the unshakable truth within.

The truth that heals,
empowers
and teaches you to love yourself first.

When you seek yourself,
you'll realize you were never lost.
You are the universe made flesh,
boundless
and radiant.

Written in the language of love,
where every breath you take
is a promise kept
and every step
brings you closer to yourself.

— The Heart of You

Being alone is not a weakness,

it does not mean you are incomplete.

It means you have the patience to wait

and the wisdom to know what you truly deserve.

You recognize your worth.

You are strong enough to build your own foundation,

to create a life that is wholly yours,

rooted in purpose, led by your truth.

The love you seek is not hidden in others

but within yourself.

A love that grows

endures

and stays with you

forever.

— Self Love

Life

The Becoming

I am sad, but I do not dwell in sorrow

I am young, but wisdom I can borrow

I am alone, but I am not lonely

I am quick, but I know how to move slowly

I am calm, but I know how to fight

I am a shadow, but I dance in the night

I am quiet, but I have much to say

I am near, but my spirit is far away

I am gentle, but my resilience is strong

I am solo, but I know how to belong

I am light, but my heart knows the dark

I am soft, but my love can leave a mark.

— I Am

Feelings can be soft and fleeting,
like a gentle nudge within,
while emotions surge like towering waves,
crashing wildly and impossible to ignore.

To embrace life's full spectrum,
we must pause, reflect, and breathe in the calm,
finding grace in both chaos and stillness,
where the heart learns to navigate.

Open the heart
to let feelings flow,
like tides pulled by an ancient moon.

Seek wisdom to guide your current
through the storm, weathering the winds,
until the clouds part
and a distant light breaks free,
illuminating the world beneath.

— Waves of Emotion

The world's rivers rush toward the ocean,
like veins carrying life to a beating heart.

The flow of life is constant,
and change
is as inevitable as the tide.

Some waves thrash against the current,
while others drift
like turtles in the swell.

Life can be unruly,
like sandstone yielding to the river's song.
Or we can let the rapids shape us smooth,
surrendering to the pull of the open sea.

. . .

THE GRAVITY OF BECOMING

When we allow ourselves to flow,
life finds ease in our embrace.

Our soul syncs with the rhythm of water,
and healing unravels
until we are weightless,
like flowers cast upon the stream.

— Go with the Flow

I gathered what was left behind—

fragments

dust

and broken bones.

Each break is a step toward wholeness,

each crack a path to strength.

From the chaos, I rise unshaken,

forged in fire and reborn from ruins.

Life stirs beneath the ash,

turning wreckage into flame.

Courage isn't given—it's earned,

woven from time lost in battle

and tears that tell the stories

of wars overcome.

We are the architects of our fate,

shaped by lessons that soften or sear,

each one moulding who we become.

. . .

THE GRAVITY OF BECOMING

Journeys unfold in strange rhythms.

Some stretch long,

others freeze in time,

yet growth thrives in the soil of struggle.

With every stumble, every fracture,

we are not breaking—we are becoming,

stepping forward to shape the life

we were always meant to create.

— Trust the Process

Let silence lead where echoes cease.

Whispers fade

when the truth is freed.

Quiet the waves of restless thought,

let stillness shape

what time forgot.

When the mind grows

as light as air,

the world unfolds—

serene and bare.

Dreams no longer drift astray—

they rise

they root

they find their way.

. . .

The veil is thin through silent space,
where all beginnings
leave no trace.

The soul is free when the spirit sings,
lifted high on unseen wings.

Where no walls remain,
and there's no weight to bear—
just presence, vivid,
raw
and rare.

Here, within the breath so deep,
silence speaks through waking sleep.

— Meditation

I rest at your feet where the tall grass bends

in the dew of morning,

where winter's breath lingers at your peak,

and the wind carries stories older than time.

Your meadows cradle the sky,

soft and golden beneath the sun's gaze,

but your ascent runs unforgiving.

Stone and silence, ice and air,

a place where only the determined dare to rise.

A river carves its path below a valley

watched by eagles circling above.

Where hikers move like shadows,

slow, deliberate, drawn upward

by a calling deeper than the climb.

. . .

THE GRAVITY OF BECOMING

Even as rocks crumble beneath their weight,

you remain unshaken—

a force too vast to be conquered,

too patient to be rushed.

I stay at your base and look beyond,

to the heights where dreams take flight,

where the earth falls away

and the soul remembers what it means to be free.

— The Mountain

Live as though
you were born with wings—
meant to defy gravity.

Spread them wide
to climb above the clouds,
where the winds of change rise.

Let them carry you
to uncharted lands,
where your heart is free
to explore endless horizons.

When night falls,
let your spirit ride the wind,
dancing through the darkness
between the stars.

— Soar

We do not change upon reaching the top.
The summit is not what defines us,
it is the climb, the shedding of weight,
the quiet unravelling of who we were.

To rise, we must transcend,
break beyond the limits of our past,
letting go of what no longer serves us
to step into the unknown.

Transcendence is not a destination
but a becoming—
a quiet shift, a hidden bloom,
an unfolding of what was always within.

Only then do we stand at the peak,
not as a product of achievement
but as a product of becoming
who we were always meant to be.

— The Breakthrough

In the deep chambers of the mind
resistance lingers like a shadowy foe,
whispering doubt
and flickering fear.

It wraps around our dreams,
making them harder to pursue,
haunting our thoughts
like an invisible force holding us back.

Yet through awareness, we regain direction.
Resistance may fuel disruption,
but remember—you control its course,
you shape your path to determine your future.

Procrastination doesn't define you,
it reveals the untapped power within—
the potential you've yet to claim
and the greatness you are destined to create.

— Beyond Resistance

Life calls through storms
and shadows,
offering lessons that slowly unfold.
It shatters your comfort,
shakes your control
and strips away what once felt whole.

You will resist,
grasping at what's known,
fearful to release
the ties that bind.

It may strike like lightning,
or whisper like a breeze,
bending your branches
and unravelling your path.

But it does not come to break you,
only to clear the way.

. . .

You may not see why the storm strips your leaves bare,

why your roots tremble.

But in time, you'll know—

these trials were not punishments

but seeds buried deep,

urging you to rise.

Through the weight of the soil,

the pull of the sun breaks through

with unwavering resolve.

And when you look back

you will see,

the hardest moments

set you free.

. . .

Life gives you what you need—

to rise

to wake up

to become.

And when you finally let go,

you will see,

the becoming was never in the answers

but in the questions, only time could reveal.

— Becoming

Isn't it strange
how so many of us fear water?

The vast depths of the ocean,
the quiet pull of a distant lake,
the wild force of a rushing river—
power we cannot control.

Make peace with water.
It is our origin,
our home before we even knew breath.

A cradle held in the womb of the world,
a sanctuary woven from love
and mystery.

A force that carries the weight of our past
and the promise of our future.

. . .

Make peace with water.

Ground your body in this world

and let your soul sink deep.

Release in the cleansing rains,

immerse in the stillness of a lake,

breathe in the salt of the ocean,

be washed clean by the river's current,

then, allow the sea

to set you free.

— Make Peace with Water

A belief is just a thought we choose to repeat.

Changing a belief takes time and courage,

but shifting a thought is within our grasp.

It's a daily practice,

a mindful choice to reshape our lives

one thought at a time.

With each thought,

we create the life we live,

a mind blooming like spring,

with energy flowing

in purpose and intention.

Change your thoughts

to reshape your world,

where manifestation rises

from within.

— Alchemy of Thoughts

If there's one truth I've learned through the years,
it's that life never stops surprising us.

The unexpected turns

the restarts

the regrets—

they're all part of the journey.

Each moment, every experience,

shapes where we are meant to be.

The universe has its way of reminding us

that nothing is ever what it seems.

Life is hard for a reason,

it's meant to test us,

challenge our resolve,

make us stronger

and push us to evolve.

When life feels too easy,

it's a sign we're not growing.

. . .

We glide through the days,
unaware of truth's sharp edges.
We search for lessons
hidden in shadows,
asking why we're here,
what we need to learn
and what we have to teach.

We didn't end up here by chance—
we chose this path,
chose the fire that would shape us,
embracing the lessons hidden in struggle.

We've prepared for these battles,
waiting for the moment
to meet ourselves,
knowing that with every scar
we carve the shape of the self
we're meant to create.

. . .

And through it all
we remember,
the greatest gift of being human
is the gift of life itself.

— Life Lesson

The sun dips below the hills as camels rest their weary legs,

diamonds paint the sky, while a story softly begs.

The sky, adorned with stars, transforms into shimmering light—

a caravan by day turns to hills of heaven by night.

The sand, an ocean of crystals and dunes,

as orange as pumpkins kissed by the moon.

The winds whisper secrets untold,

spoken by a young boy whose soul is old.

To the nomad whose words changed my view,

stars danced to your stories under the new moon.

You spoke of your past, of wandering sheep,

trading for riches and food you could keep.

Like a living Santiago from Andalusia's land,

you searched for your treasure with no home at hand.

No family, no name, or age to be known,

you longed for a place to call your own.

. . .

From that night in the desert,
I'll never be the same.
Like an angel guiding,
you showed me the way.

A life of wandering, untamed and free,
embracing the stars as they showed what could be.
Under a blanket of constellations, lighting the night,
came healing from scars, and darkness turned bright.

To that evening in the desert, I carry its flame
into a bright future where I'll never be the same.
With wonder as my compass and stars lighting the way,
I'll never forget the magic discovered that day.

In the stillness of night, with the soft sandy sway,
the spirit of the desert will forever stay.

— Sahara

Just as nature moves in an eternal dance
we glide through the seasons of life,
swaying with the universe's pulse
like tides drawn by the moon's hand.

We meet endless beginnings
and endless farewells,
yet we mourn what slips from our grasp.
Nothing lasts forever—
still, we cling to the hope of eternity.

For every dawn, there's a dusk,
sorrow shifts to joy
and laughter fades to tears.
Neither joy nor grief stays the same.

Failure rises, only to be eclipsed by triumph,
and champions can fall from grace.
All things come to an end.

. . .

Let this stir anticipation

for what waits beyond the horizon,

the next cycle, the new beginning.

Embrace the ebb and flow of existence,

breathe in the pulse of life—

birth, decay, death

and the quiet rebirth that follows.

This is the rhythm that never ceases.

Flow with the universe,

honouring the cycles that shape us

through an eternal dance of becoming.

— Life Cycle

Knowledge flows in vibrant shades,

a spectrum of ideas,

bold and ever-changing.

But in stillness,

wisdom glows, steady and bright,

illuminating the path that guides the night.

Knowledge paints the world,

filling the mind with depth and emotion.

Wisdom clears the fog,

casting clarity where meaning takes root.

One speaks in colour, the other in light.

Knowledge is learned,

while wisdom is earned.

— Insights

Trust the part of you
that knows
there is more beyond now.

Your inner voice is a compass,
pulling you forward
toward the life waiting to unfold.

Listen closely to that quiet pull,
the whisper that reminds you
the universe is alive with doors
only you can open.

— Potential

Allow yourself to dream without limits,

to see beyond what is

and into what could be.

Believe you are worthy

of a life rich in joy

fulfillment

and purpose.

Trust yourself

and the path will unfold,

a journey of growth

discovery

and dreams made real.

— Possibilities

THE GRAVITY OF BECOMING

Each chapter that closes is not an end
but an invitation to begin again,
a chance to embrace new possibilities
free from the weight of the past.

What lies ahead
often holds more promise
than what we've left behind.

In the space between
endings and beginnings,
growth unfolds.

Through reinvention, we discover
that every ending
marks the start
of something new.

— Turn the Page

If we don't make our bodies
a cradle for the light,
we risk sinking into darkness.

The light we carry within
grounds us,
in balance and alignment.

To embrace positivity,
we must face its shadow,
acknowledging its role
in life's grand design.

Only through awareness
can we honour our light
within our darkness.

. . .

Transforming shadows

into deeper understanding

and rising anew with each dawn,

like the moon giving way to the sun.

— Duality

Empathy is the cornerstone

of human connection,

a bridge between hearts

where silence speaks the truth.

It calls us to step beyond ourselves,

so we can see through another's eyes,

acknowledging their pain

and honouring their experience.

In a world where judgment clouds the heart,

nurturing kindness is essential

to build a stronger, gentler community.

By embracing empathy,

we create a wave,

shifting lives

one connection at a time.

— The Links of Us

It begins with a willingness
to learn from another's journey,
to truly listen and understand the richness
of their experience.

When we nurture curiosity and dialogue,
we free ourselves from preconceived notions
and rise above stereotypes,
shattering barriers
and dissolving stigma.

This mindset builds bridges,
uniting hearts, communities,
and cultures.

In the end, it creates a world
where connection and mutual respect
can thrive.

— Through Another's Eyes

When you truly understand the question,
the answer is already within you.
Clarity isn't something to search for outside,
it's something to uncover from within.

All the wisdom,
guidance
and insights you seek
are woven into the fabric of your soul.

The answers to life's questions
aren't hidden in the world around you
but in the stillness within,
where your inner voice speaks your truth.

Let it guide you—
it holds the key to all you seek,
the path to becoming
all you're meant to be.

— Universal Truth

THE GRAVITY OF BECOMING

In this moment
there is no seeking,
no sorrow
no hoping, no wishing,
no memories lingering,
no thoughts of tomorrow.

There is no time passing,
no clock ticking.

This moment is all that is,
and I am
the silence that holds all noise,
the pulse of existence
and the breath of eternity.
I am...

— Peace

We are a reflection

of the company we keep.

The people we surround ourselves with

shape our thoughts,

our behaviours and our worldview,

often in ways subtle yet profound.

Strength is not in appearing balanced

while chaos swirls.

Peace is not found by merging with disorder.

It is earned by cultivating relationships

and environments

that breathe calm into your soul.

. . .

In a world overwhelmed by distractions and noise, seek connections that elevate your spirit.

Let these bonds be a lighthouse, guiding you through the storm toward the shores of peace.

— Energy of Influence

Get comfortable with discomfort,
it is the fertile soil
where growth takes root.

The only authentic way to evolve
is through the only constant in life—
change.

Change is unpredictable,
often unsettling
yet always essential.

It pushes us beyond
the boundaries of what we know,
challenging us to explore
new possibilities.

. . .

Embrace discomfort,
within it lies strength,
resilience
and the capacity to transform
in the face of uncertainty.

The unease you face today
becomes the foundation
of who you'll be tomorrow.

— Edge of Expansion

Your body is a mirror

to your mind.

Reflecting every thought

you nurture.

Fill it with negativity,

worry

or toxicity

and your body will bear the weight,

manifesting pain, illness

or unrest.

But when positivity

and peace resides within

your body follows,

unfolding in harmony and health.

. . .

In this stillness,

light exists everywhere

and nowhere,

where every fear and every worry

is gently lifted from your being.

A space beyond words,

where love has no beginning or end,

where presence is both familiar

and infinite.

Here, the soul dances freely

in the embrace of eternity,

where time dissolves

and all that remains

is the eternal pulse of presence.

— Transcendence

At the threshold, energy flows
as a bridge between realms.
Channelling brilliance from above
to transform thought into action.

One hand reaches upward,
drawing down the light of stars,
while the other stays grounded,
rooted deep in the pulse of the earth.

In this stillness, power stirs within
wands, cups, swords, and coins—
symbols of possibility
waiting to be awakened.

The power to shape desire and destiny
dwells within,
calling us to build the life
we want to create.

. . .

As above, so below.

The ancients whisper the truth

reflected through the sky.

Step into your magic,

life is a stage

waiting for you to manifest your show.

— The Magician

In the embrace of lush mountains

where ancient guardians stretch toward the sky,

the air hums with the rich aroma of coffee beans

buried deep in the earth's embrace.

Each breath carries the weight of untold stories,

a promise of a life yet to unfold.

Among towering eucalyptus trees

the colours pulse, revealing the earth's secrets.

Solace rests in the leaves,

while refuge lies in the roots,

where spirits beckon to be awakened.

Monkeys play in the canopies,

with laughter dancing on the breeze,

while sloths glide slowly through the trees.

The ocean calls with rhythmic waves,

its voice carried through to shore,

while sunlight bathes the day in warmth.

. . .

Here, meditation flows like a gentle stream,

merging with the vastness of existence,

while yoga stretches the soul to the rhythm of the land,

uniting body and spirit in peace and prosperity.

This is where the mind is set free,

the spirit rediscovered, restored and reborn.

Where earth and sky,

body and mind, intertwine

through a sacred dance of renewal.

— Costa Rica

Where the sea kisses the shore
and the wind carries whispers
from distant lands,
the islands vibrate with timeless energy,
as the sand holds traces of forgotten stories—
like a message in a bottle drifting out to sea.

Vibrant streets hum with life,
bathed in golden glow,
while the air dances with salt
and flowers bloom below.

Beneath the emerald canopy,
mangroves curl like hidden secrets
and dolphins carve through crystal waters
like freedom in motion.

. . .

THE GRAVITY OF BECOMING

Time slows,

blending peace with adventure,

inviting surrender to the wild beauty

of land and sea.

A place for souls to awaken,

where the pulse of the ocean stirs the spirit,

and turquoise depths call for transformation.

Through the call, the self dissolves—

every ripple beckons you deeper.

Until the world above and the depths below surrender,

and you become one with the tide.

— Bocas del Toro

Healing is a non-linear journey,
a process of unfolding
that defies time and expectation.

It is not a straight path
but a series of twists,
turns
and unexpected pauses.

Progress often hides in the unseen
and setbacks carve their own way forward.

Healing calls to the brave—
to face discomfort and uncertainty,
to surrender to the unravelling
of the familiar.

. . .

Through healing,
we discover strength we never knew we had,
and the resilience to rise again,
even when the way is unclear.

Healing is not for the faint of heart,
it is for those willing to endure,
grow
and transform.

— Mending

Carve a clearing

in the dense forest of your life,

then stand in the stillness

and wait

until your story gently settles at your feet.

You are not meant

to carry the weight of the world

but to tend to the fire within,

to nourish, to listen,

to let your soul breathe.

In the quiet wisdom rises like dawn,

soft but certain,

calling you to step forward,

to offer your light.

Rise and heal,

to step into the fullness of your becoming.

— Purpose

Clean thoughts
are the garden where a vibrant,
purposeful life takes root,
nourishing the mind
and strengthening the foundation
of your being.

The state of your body
reflects the energy of your thoughts,
and within that power
lies the potential for radical transformation.

Release the clutter of negativity
and watch clarity bloom.
In the peace of a mind freed,
the path to transformation becomes undeniable
and you become the force that shapes your path.

— Cleanse

In the embrace of sandstone buildings

where earth meets azure sky,

I wander through vibrant souks

with air thick in the scent of spice.

Among the ancient medina,

teaching becomes a dance,

cross-cultural hearts

form bridges across barren lands.

Beneath the shade of a palm tree,

I meet a soul who speaks in silence,

each gesture a fragile gift,

a window into his world unspoken.

We flow through currents of communication,

direct yet subtle,

where laughter rises like a call to prayer,

reverberating through the golden air.

. . .

THE GRAVITY OF BECOMING

Here lies a land of contrasts,
where donkeys pull carts
and sports cars race
down bustling streets.

In the city, alleys cradle the night
with roads bathed in pools of light.
The Adhan echoes five times a day,
a call to stillness on display.

In the country, winding roads ascend,
where gemstones sit untouched by time.
The High Atlas fades into the Sahara's embrace,
silence stretching beyond infinite space.

Across the world, over an ocean,
another home away from home to embrace,
offering sights to see and dreams to chase,
unfolding like a map, discovering new layers of me.

— Morocco

When words escape you

and silence fills your space,

turn to your art.

It holds the key

to unlock your truth—

in every stroke,

every colour,

every movement

or every note.

Let your heart weave stories,

let your soul carve its path.

Art shouts the truths

that words can't speak,

when silence swallows sound

and your voice is out of reach.

— Let Your Art Speak

There is no greater guide
than death's touch,
leading us towards the light.

From its shadow, a revival stirs,
a spark ignites, rising bold and bright,
pulling us from the dark into the dawn.

In the stillness of the storm
we uncover truths once veiled,
finding strength in the gentle breeze
to discover how far we can sail.

— The Reawakening

There's a voice that speaks without sound
a quiet pull, both deep and profound.
It calls when the path feels unclear,
a steady presence, always near.

It's the ember in the wind, the moonlight at night,
a spark of truth that cuts through the fight.
When logic clouds the road ahead
this silent wisdom is where you're led.

It's a feeling that can't be named
an inner compass, wild and untamed.
It doesn't shout nor seek to prove
but gently whispers of your next move.

Trust it when the world grows loud,
it's clarity through the crowd.
In moments of doubt, when hope feels thin
this quiet strength will pull you within.

— Intuition

THE GRAVITY OF BECOMING

Strangers met while travelling
are best friends in disguise,
sharing fleeting moments
beneath endless skies.

On crowded trains and bustling streets
we find connection in passing beats,
a knowing glance
a fleeting smile
a quiet magic shared for a while.

In every face there's a trace of home
where miles fade and hearts can roam.

Though paths may part
the bond remains
a moment in time—
only friendship
can claim.

— Kindred

I've shed the skin that ruled my heart,

replaced with compassion

for a brand new start.

New blooms unwind in the garden of time,

but in the lake, there's a glimpse

of the wild-eyed dreamer—

the inner child present

through every wake of change.

She lets down her hair

with laughter and longing,

as each passing season

gathers grace and belonging.

In every new reflection

there's an invitation

from the unknown,

a call to venture on.

. . .

THE GRAVITY OF BECOMING

Forging ahead

while honouring the past,

as the woman who walks

holding the girl who has surpassed.

Down by the water

another skin is shed.

Through the ripples of time,

introspection spreads,

where reflections reveal

the new me ahead.

— Identity Shift

Your pyramids haunt my dreams,

whispering secrets

on the desert's breath,

lingering spirits of pharaohs

stretch endlessly across the sand.

The Nile winds through my veins,

a river of forgotten memories

carrying the stories

etched in my bones,

weaving ancient paths

through waters unknown.

Dunes rise

vast and eternal,

reaching toward the sacred land

where temples stand defiant

beneath the sun,

and walls breathe life

into legends of glory.

. . .

THE GRAVITY OF BECOMING

The Sphinx stands tall,
a silent guardian of untold dreams,
its gaze unyielding
and wise,
whispering in a language
older than time.

Every step on this hallowed ground
carries the weight
of centuries.

The breath of the past
stirs in the air,
a quiet reminder of who I was,
who I am
and why I am meant to return.

— Egypt

Some truths are unspeakable
hidden even from the light.
Thoughts can tangle in the dark,
lost within the night.

But each flicker of feeling,
every whisper of the soul,
is a story waiting to break free,
to heal, and make us whole.

With ink as your refuge
pour out what you've kept,
transforming silence into sound,
giving life to what's been swept.

Every stroke is a release
every verse is a breath,
in the pages of your truth,
find life beyond death.

. . .

Let the words flow wild,

unshackled, unafraid,

this sacred space

is where creativity is made.

In every line you write

the world becomes your stage—

to speak

to dream

and ignite a new age.

— The Pages of You

You wander through a house of glass,

burdened by weights

too heavy to last.

You try to shift the world

but miss the truth that lies within—

the shattered reflection

that will set you free.

Life reflects what you dare to see,

a house of mirrors

infinite and free.

To see beyond, you must let go,

surrender to the peace

you long to know.

You are not the only soul stuck here,

countless others

are lost in fear.

. . .

Chasing illusions that bind your mind,
tangled in chains
that never unwind.

Let go of the ties that hold you tight
and the walls you built
to dim your light.

True change blooms from a quiet place,
found only in the peace
that you can create.

— House of Mirrors

Every summer, I rejoice

in the warm embrace of the breeze,

listening to the birds' melodies

while basking in sunlight.

With each fall, I prepare for my demise,

letting my leaves transform,

releasing their grip from branches once adored.

Yielding to the cold,

becoming a quiet tomb,

shrouded in snow and ice.

In winter, I hibernate,

sinking into the stillness of the earth,

reflecting its tranquil mirror.

Pondering the seasons of change,

while grounding lessons

from the year now past.

. . .

Every spring, I awaken,
bearing winter's scars
but inhaling the fragrance of new blooms,
opening my soul to warmth once more.

A tender leaf grows on a budding branch,
part of a vibrant new tree.
Each season affirming my place,
my growth, my return
to the evolving cycle of life.

And as I embrace the change
I know this truth,
life is constantly unfolding
in a dance of what was
what is
and what will be.

— Like the Trees

I was gifted a son who doesn't sleep,

so I could rise to meet myself.

The self that awakens in the stillness of midnight,

where the creative spirit breaks free,

like a great horned owl.

Wings stretch wide in the shadows,

eyes gleam with wisdom

and wildness.

In this quiet rise, ideas take flight,

unfolding in the peace

where the soul roams free

from the tick of time's grip.

. . .

The midnight muse calls not with words
but with knowing—
whispering stories in the cool night air.

A reminder that creation rises with the moon,
and I
am a channel,
alive in the dark,
shifting through the stars in the wake of the moon.

Merging with the stillness of night,
a dance drifting between shadows and light.

— The Nocturnal Muse

Eyes speak through vibrant hues
in visions vast and deep,
where the secrets of the universe
wait for those bold enough to seek.

As the journey unfolds,
they watch with silent grace,
bathed in an unspoken glow
where time dissolves without a trace.

Through their depth,
worlds begin to converge,
a quiet knowing stirs
as truth begins to emerge.

They carry a map of stardust,
guiding us through celestial trails,
a silent calling
urging us to wander where dreams prevail.

. . .

Through their silence

an inner storm awakens,

stirring across distant skies,

unveiling realms unseen

where the soul finds refuge to rise.

It's there in the subtle shine,

in every open eye,

a universe of endless possibilities,

where mind

body

and soul

dare to touch the sky.

— Windows to the Soul

Who you are is not your body,

not your mind, nor this fleeting lifetime.

You are the witness, the breeze in the trees,

the deer in the forest, the moose in the snow.

You are not the life you've built,

nor the job that binds you.

You are the river's flow,

the clouds drifting in the sky.

You are not the thoughts that race,

nor the friends you've lost or left behind.

You are the grass in open fields

and the birds soaring free.

You are the diver in the deep

and the swimmer breaking the surface.

You are everything and nothing,

all at once.

. . .

And when you remember this,
you will know that you are the heartbeat of the earth,
the spark of the stars,
the breath of the universe itself.

You are infinite energy
flowing through consciousness,
unbound by time,
unburdened by the world.

— Soul Self

We weave our world with careful hands,

shaping structures we call our own,

through beliefs, routines, and walls we build,

until they harden into stone.

We mistake the mask for the maker,

the echoes for the voice within,

forgetting we are not what's forged

but the forgers—free to begin.

Yet comfort clings like tangled roots

binding us to what we know,

afraid to tear the old away,

to let uncertainty help us grow.

But when we loosen our tightened grip,

the world unfolds with a vast embrace.

In releasing, we create space for more,

and what fades becomes fertile ground for grace.

— Artisans of Growth

Epilogue

These words are fragments of my heart, pieces of a story still unfolding. Life moves like the tide, weaving loss, love, joy, and sorrow in ways I am still learning to understand.

This is not an ending but an invitation to reflect, feel, and embrace the changing landscape of your journey. These pages hold my experiences, but they also belong to you. They are a mirror, a reminder that you are never alone in both the beauty and the pain.

Healing is not linear. It moves like the seasons—sometimes slow and aching, other times sudden and wild. Through every tear, every quiet breath, every step forward, we bloom and rise again.

As you turn these final pages, may these words be a light along the way. There is resilience in you, strength in you, and infinite possibility in every new beginning.

Even in the darkest moments, may you always dare to reach for the stars.

With love,

Kelsey

"We are all broken, that's how the light gets in."

— Ernest Hemingway

About the Author

Kelsey Pilling is a writer and holistic health practitioner committed to helping others cultivate deep healing, self-discovery, and personal transformation. With an integrative method that combines mind, body, and spirit, she empowers individuals to navigate life's complexities with resilience, authenticity, and compassion.

Nestled in the Foothills of Alberta, Canada, Kelsey shares a vibrant life with her family of six. Living on a peaceful acreage, she draws inspiration from nature's rhythms, finding peace in the mountains, wisdom in the stars, and solace in the changing seasons. Grounded in mindfulness, Kelsey's approach to wellness embraces the truth that healing arises when we surrender to vulnerability, welcome acceptance, and flow with change.

Through her work and writing, Kelsey invites others to fully embrace their journey, moving through love, loss, and transformation with an open heart. She believes life's depth and beauty are found in presence, perspective, and the ability to find light in every moment.

Discover more about Kelsey's transformative coaching and healing work at www.kelseypilling.com.

Manufactured by Amazon.ca
Acheson, AB

16676168R00114